BASHFULNESS CURED

LECTOR HOUSE PUBLIC DOMAIN WORKS

BASHFULNESS CURED

ANONYMOUS

ISBN: 978-93-90294-55-8

Published: 1872.

LECTOR HOUSE LLP
E-MAIL: lectorpublishing@gmail.com

BASHFULNESS CURED:

EASE AND ELEGANCE
OF MANNER QUICKLY GAINED.

BY

ANONYMOUS

1872.

CONTENTS

BASHFULNESS—DIFFIDENCE.—DEFINITION.

We do not see why Sidney should have termed *diffidence* "rustic shame." Very many nice and proper persons who live in rural parts, and who are exceedingly bashful, are far from being shame-faced. "Excessive or extreme modesty," Webster defines bashfulness, and this is the better definition, though not literally correct, as many who are rough, impudent and vulgar in the privacy of their own homes, are wretchedly bashful when in company of strangers, or those whom they consider their superiors.

No emotion is more painful than bashfulness. Without feeling guilty, its subject feels crushed. Says one, "I am troubled with a painful sense of timidity and bashfulness in the presence of company on being spoken to, especially at the table; and no matter whether the person be my equal or my inferior, I blush from the cravat to the hair, and the very consciousness that I am blushing, and that my embarrassment is discovered, tends to deepen the blush and heighten the embarrassment. Now, I have a good personal appearance; I have a good education; I occupy a good position in society; I have been trusted by my friends with official position, and feel myself competent to fill it, and when I sit down to meditate I feel no cause for embarrassment or bashfulness; I can converse for hours with persons of culture and superior ability, and feel no cause of shame at the part I am enabled to act; still, if then spoken to suddenly or abruptly, this terrible diffidence comes upon me like a spell, and makes me stammer; my head seems splitting with excitement; my face turns red; my heart palpitates, and I am no longer, for the moment, myself. Now all this is very distressing." Yes, this is distressing, as very many can testify from disagreeable experience.

There are many influences that may directly and indirectly be mentioned as being the

CAUSES OF BASHFULNESS.

Among them is a certain peculiarity of constitution known as *"natural diffidence;"* then, *bashfulness from ignorance of the ways of society; lack of education; ill-dress; ill-health; nervousness.*

NATURAL DIFFIDENCE.

How to acquire Elegance and Fluency of Expression—Ease and Polish of Manner—a Graceful, Pleasing and Dignified Bearing—a Handsome Well-developed Chest—a Deep, Rich Voice. How to Dress Cheaply and Elegantly—How to be Attractive by certain attentions to Personal Habits. To the Debilitated: what to use to become Strong (new). How to Please greatly by delicate Flattery of Eye and Manner. A Secret of being Popular with the Ladies. How to easily Train, Brighten, and Sharpen the Intellect. To be Well-informed and Well-cultivated

Many persons are constitutionally timid and diffident. They were bashful in childhood, bashful at school, bashful in society, always bashful. In business they are not generally your pushing, go-ahead operators. They shrink from contact with the bustling crowds. They prefer, and will usually be found doing quiet brain work in dim back offices.

Bashful young ladies, to the rightly constituted masculine mind, are rather attractive than otherwise. The timid, retiring manner; the modest, downcast look; the soft blushes—all are particularly engaging, especially to those who have been long in society, and accustomed to the cool self-possession and calm assurance of fashionable ladies.

The genuine diffident girl is not the product of cities. She is not found in the crash of town life, but in the seclusion of quiet country towns.

There is no class of girls in the world so easy to get along with after they get acquainted with you, as bashful ones. And the courting them is an easy and delightful affair; they are so loving and confiding; no reserve, no distrust, no coquetting; but frank, open-hearted and generous. Even if you are unsuccessful in your suit they never mortify you in their refusal. It is generally given in so frank and candid a manner as to command your admiration.

Natural Diffidence is the result, as already stated, of certain peculiarities of constitution. There is a want of confidence in one's self—a shrinking dread of intercourse with strangers, especially those of the opposite sex, and he, or she, can give no reason for this diffident feeling. He may be well educated; of attractive personal appearance, of good conversational abilities, and well dressed, yet from that strange feeling of natural bashfulness, so well known, yet difficult to describe, he is a timid, shrinking creature, subject to trials of which a self-reliant man has no conception. He blushes and becomes confused if suddenly addressed. His heart beats painfully at the idea of entering a well-lighted room filled with ladies and gentlemen. And this feeling is the result, in a great measure, of his small *self-esteem*. Your truly diffident person is of extremely sensitive, retiring disposition, and while he is apt to accord to others superiorities they do not possess, he entertains for his own abilities, personal and mental qualities, the most humble opinion. And thus he does himself great injustice and injury. He does not attain that position in society nor that success in professional or business life that he would were he not shackled by his foolish timidity—his deference to others.

A bold, self-confident man, with a mere fraction of a bashful man's ability and attainments, will invariably distance him in the affairs of life. "Brass" always tells. The world don't stop to analyze a man for his real merit. It takes him at his own valuation, and if a man puts a low estimate upon himself and goes through life with a hanging head and blushing face, he has small success, and less pity. The good things of this world—the successes in love, in business, in politics, &c., are invariably won by those who have a good opinion of themselves; who have faith in their special talents and abilities, and who push ahead in accordance with this faith.

There never was a truer saying than that faint heart never won fair lady. While women have a genuine admiration for the truly modest and pure-minded men, they have a genuine contempt for your chicken-hearted, bashful, tongue-tied fellows.

Although a good many screeching females in these Women's Rights, Advanced Female days can not lay special claims to any superfluous amount of modesty, still the softer sex have not yet lost those endearing qualities of gentleness, modesty, and loving trustfulness in the opposite sex. Since that time when Eve cast her first loving glances towards robust Adam, women's love and admiration have gone out to bold and gallant men. As she is timid and weak, so the more does she admire the qualities of strength and courage. Man is her natural protector, and she looks up to him and clings to him in love and confidence.

Women are pre-eminently romantic in all that concerns love. Her heroes are those who do brave and perilous deeds; who scorn ease and effeminacy, and who laugh at danger—captains who go down to the sea in ships and sail away over the mysterious ocean to strange, far-away lands—men who with shut jaws, gleaming eyes, and fixed bayonets go digging over fort walls, from which come unceasing flashes of fire and a pitiless rain of death.

(How the officers and men who came home from The War were honored, and almost caressed, especially by the ladies; and what a host of marriages took place among the gallant fellows!)

It has been truly said that no woman really loves who has not discovered some traits in her lover's character that she considers noble and heroic. It is a glory for a woman to be able to be proud of her lover or husband—of his superior intellect, his dignity and strong manhood and loving care and tenderness, and it is proverbial how a true woman overlooks and endeavors to conceal the faults and weaknesses of her husband. He was her hero at marriage, and though the illusion may have passed, she still bravely tries to maintain it.

It often happens that a bright, superior girl marries a quiet, bashful fellow, in whom her friends do not see anything worth marrying for. But it is certain the girl has discovered under all the young man's reserve and diffidence, superior traits of character that have secured her attention and love.

This may be illustrated by an incident in which the actors are personally known to the writer.

Frank W—— was a young man of more than common intelligence and strength of character, but he was so obstinately bashful and retiring that his real worth was entirely unappreciated by his acquaintances. He rarely ventured out to parties, &c., and when he did, was entirely eclipsed by all the ready-tongued young men in the room. Now this Frank W—— was irretrievably in love with the most charming young lady in town, Miss Louisa L——, who understood and appreciated W——, and often gave his society marked preference, to the surprise and disgust of the before-mentioned ready-tongued fellows, yet was careful to give no indication by which W— — could hope he had secured her affections. Thus matters went on a couple of years, and W— — was almost in despair, though he had really made more progress than he had imagined. But an accident occurred that brought matters to an agreeable termination. They were out for a ride, with a spirited horse one autumn afternoon, and in going down a steep hill a rein broke, and the animal dashed forward at a tremendous pace. W— — turned quietly towards Miss L— —, and giving her an assuring look, placed a foot on the dasher-board, and with a leap placed himself fairly astride the animal. Leaning forward and seizing the beast by the nostrils he twisted her head suddenly to one side, and brought the whole affair to a stand-still within half-a-dozen rods. Soothing the excited horse by a little gentle stroking, W— — united the rein, and then coolly drove on as if nothing had happened.

"I then and there decided to marry him," said Miss L— —, relating the incident. "I concluded that one who could perform such a daring and dangerous act, and regard it with quiet indifference, was a true and noble man, and one whom I could implicitly trust." And she was right, for a woman never secured a better or more faithful husband.

A bashful young man who had the appearance of no great amount of spirit, complained to his father of his want of success in winning the esteem of a certain proud young lady. "You can swim, Sam?" "Yes, sir." "Well, the next time you go sailing with that girl, manage to dip her into the stream, without letting her suspect you; then rescue her like a man. Or do anything else that will show that you have some life and pluck, and you'll find she has an improved opinion of you directly."

And the pith of wisdom is in this bit of paternal advice.

Rather than be a bashful, blushing, stuttering booby, it would be much better for a young man to be over-confident and bold. With the latter qualities his chances of success in any direction in life, would be infinitely better. And it is the stout, true heart that finds favor with the ladies. Women love to be sought, and have attention paid them. It is their nature to be timid, trustful and confiding. They love to rely upon and feel the support of manly strength. Now a timid, bashful fellow does not possess those qualities that women most admire, and to possess them should be a bashful person's foremost ambition.

The boy who hangs his head and sucks his thumb when spoken to by a stranger, and who is generally to be found moping behind the kitchen fire, looking at a picture book, is not the mother's favorite. The saucy little chap who sticks his fists into his breeches pocket, and don't see anything in strangers to fear; who rides the colts bare-back; who don't like the girls because they can't climb after bird's eggs; who sails about the pond on a six foot plank; and is the leader in all kinds of boyish mischief;—this is the brave and fearless boy that fills his mother's heart with secret pride and joy. "The spunky little cuss," though coarse and jarring, is far more pleasant to the mother's ear than "Poor child, he is so sensitive and bashful."

NOT BASHFUL.

And again we repeat, women do not admire bashful men. While they may pity, a woman secretly despises a man who is really or appears to be *afraid of women*. A diffident fellow never was nor never will be a favorite with the ladies. It is your easy-going, self-possessed, talking chaps who are the popular ones. This is illustrated in any assemblage of both sexes. Take a party, for instance, early in the evening when matters are a little frigid. The ladies are inclined to congregate in groups by themselves, with shy glances towards the gentlemen, whose inclinations seem to be that of making wall-ornaments of themselves. Presently there will enter the room a fellow who is not quite certain if he understands what the word "bashfulness" means. He goes up to a group of ladies, smiles and bows to all, shakes hands with some, and is in felicity right away, to the envy and admiration of the wall-ornament chaps.

While young ladies are timid and retiring, they dislike the exhibition of these qualities by men. This cannot be better illustrated than by noticing how a young man from the city, with his easy manners, his self-assurance, and ready ways, will go into a country village and "cut out" the fellows right and left, making himself a favorite with the girls in an amazing short time. And this fellow may be only a shallow-brained fop from some city dry goods store, where he is engaged measuring out ribbons from 8 A. M. till 6 P. M. His education is not worth speaking of; he smokes; he gets drunk making New Year's calls; he don't go to church; his moral character will not bear severe inspection, and yet this fellow goes to the country, and even the sensible girls rather admire him, and are well pleased to see him coming up the walk for an evening's visit. The best of the country beaux have received a good education at the academy; they are clear in head and sound in body, they are able to marry, owning their own business, or soon to do so, and yet the company of a pop-in-jay chap from the city is openly preferred to that of these substantial and worthy country young men. And they do not understand it, though it is plain enough. The city fellow brings with him an air of the great world outside this country village. For years he has read the morning paper as regularly as he has taken his breakfast, therefore he is informed of all the events of the day. He can tell you the present mental condition of Queen Victoria, what the latest news is from Mormondom, or how Prince Jim Jund is progressing with his railroad enterprise in Africa. He can discuss politics with the father, talk with mother concerning the last General Religious Convention, and with the young ladies fairly effervesces with small talk. And here he has at immense advantage the country young men, whose current literature probably consists of the Weekly County paper, fearfully dry and dull, a city story, or Agricultural paper, and Ayre's last Almanac. With these only for his mental food, how can a young man make himself entertaining and agreeable with chatty talk on the light topics of the day?

The city chap is brim full of pleasant gossip. He don't sit cross-legged, twisting his hat and talking tedious farm-talk to the "old man," while he is dying to be visiting with the women-folks.

He has long been in contact with people—the world—and constant friction has rubbed out any awkwardness he may have possessed years ago. There is an agreeable ease and freedom in his manner, as there is in that of all genuine city people, and it could not well be otherwise. In his capacity of salesman in a large city retail store, he has come in contact with all classes of ladies. He don't blush now when addressed by one of them. The sight of bright eyes and pretty ankles does not throw him into a state of flutteration, as it does our country friend. He isn't afraid of the women much—not much. He does not class them with the angel species, to converse with whom requires great courage and moral force. He has learned by considerable unpleasant experience that a great many of the gentler sex have brisk little tempers, and some spiteful, harassing ways, and tongues that can say sharp things:—in fact, who are very much mortal, and so, not considering them either doves or angels, he experiences no trepidation in their society whatever.

Again, our city fellow, rusticating in the country, and having it very much his own way with the damsels, is *well dressed*. His clothes are probably not of expensive material, but they are of excellent fit, and gives his person a stylish, genteel appearance.

That a person well dressed receives respect and attention that would not possibly be shown him were he poorly or slovenly clothed is a fact so familiar to all that it would be absurd to discuss it.

The matter of Dress is of so much importance as concerns the feeling of *Bashfulness*, that we shall consider it fully in another chapter.

THE CURE OF NATURAL BASHFULNESS.

Consists:—1. *In cultivating* Self-Esteem,—*in exalting your own opinion of yourself.* Being Proud.

2. *Going into company;—associating with miscellaneous people.*

1. Who ever knew a really proud person to be bashful and diffident? What is pride? Is it not self-esteem; self-appreciation and valuation; self-respect and reliance; nobleness, independence and dignity?

A proud-spirited person excites in us something of that feeling of respect and admiration we have for a spirited, mettlesome horse.

But to possess true spirit and personal pride, we must possess points of real or imagined merit; of education, accomplishments, personal beauty, or mental, or physical superiority. How can a person of scanty information—ignorant of the world and its doings, carry a proud bearing with a high and noble spirit?

"How proud and stuck up them Brown girls are since they got home from Boston," whispers Mrs. Smith to a neighbor, as the "Brown girls" sail into church, dressed in city style, and with something of "city airs." They have brought home with them the same warm, generous hearts—but they are proud. Have they not some reason for being so? For two years they have been in Madame C.'s fashionable city boarding-school, and in this time they have learned several things outside their school books. Their rustic ways quickly disappeared, and they soon acquired quiet dignity of manners, and that perfect self-control we all admire. It was taught them also that the face is not the proper place for exhibiting our emotions and feelings, so often to our disadvantage; and also that the "sweet, low voice" that men love so well, is much more effective than the loud, harsh tones of so many rustic maidens.

They were also trained to receive introductions from gentlemen without simpering and blushing, and also that it was possible for a gentleman to call upon them several times, and even invite them to a concert, and still have no intentions of "proposing."

And so the Brown girls go home with their varied accomplishments, and are "proud." But it is a personal pride to be approved of, and which all who are bashful and backward should strive to acquire.

Are you ambitious? Do you aspire to better things? If you consider yourself a nobody, do you care to be somebody? Do you care to be considered an intelligent, interesting capable person? Then analyze yourself; take yourself to pieces, and see what there is really of you. We take it for granted, of course, that you are a person of ordinary common sense. Has your school education been neglected? then you must rectify this by a selected course of reading; for the first and most important step towards removing a feeling of bashfulness and inferiority, is to become well informed on general topics. We maintain that it is absurd for any intelligent person to feel awkward and bashful who is well-informed and neatly dressed.

To make up for deficiencies of education, any person determined can go through a special course of reading in a comparatively short time, that will make him or her a well informed person. The books we would particularly recommend, are:—A concise Modern History; a small Ancient History; Natural Philosophy (Comstock's High School, or any other good, well illustrated work); Youman's New Chemistry, which you will find very interesting and highly instructive; Quackenbos' Composition and Rhetoric. If you read carefully Kame's Elements of Criticism you would be richly repaid in the pleasure derived, and in the gain of a rich store of valuable information. Any person who would be pre-eminently quick-witted must not fail to read Shakespeare—at least the principal plays. Shakespeare's knowledge of the world—of the secret springs of human action—of *human nature*—was something wonderful. No human being has yet equalled him in this respect. But you cannot read his plays as you can a newspaper. They must be slowly read and digested like a rare dinner. The Bible perhaps excepted, no book has yet been printed that contains so great an amount of profound worldly wisdom as the works of Shakespeare. Nothing will so quickly sharpen and polish a dull and untrained intellect.

Now here are enumerated less than a dozen books, within the reach of any one capable of earning his clothes, and which, if read at least twice, carefully, will make a person feel that he really knows something—had really entered the great temple of knowledge.

Of course, one should not be confined to the above. The extent of one's intelligence and information will depend upon the extent of his reading and thinking; but the above-mentioned books, thoroughly read, will educate and elevate more than the perusal of an entire library read hastily and thoughtlessly.

The wide range of information gained by the regular perusal of a good city daily newspaper, and a first class monthly magazine is of too great value to be over-estimated. If you cannot afford a daily paper, you certainly can a semi-weekly, a large one, like the Semi-Weekly Tribune, for instance. Of the magazines, *Harper's* or *Scribner's* will bring you treasures of interesting knowledge in the most attractive form.

We will now suppose that you are well informed of the news and topics of the day, etc., and that you have no cause to feel diffident and reserved from a general lack of information. "But my self-esteem is small, I have a poor opinion of myself." Well, change that opinion! Be proud; resolve to walk like a MAN and a gentleman—not like an uncouth boy. Hold up your head, and throw back your shoulders. If you want a magnificent chest, and a deep, sonorous voice; practice ten minutes, night and morning, filling the lungs as full as possible through a small tube, three inches long, and with a hole the size of a quill; allow the breath to pass out slowly through the tube. To insure an easy and graceful carriage, practice walking in your room with a small bag filled with grain poised on your head. Consider yourself as good as other people, *and a little better*. Train yourself to act always in a quiet and dignified manner—not with vulgar "stiffness," but with that ease and moderation of action, easily acquired, and which always shows the well-bred person. *Act* the gentleman or lady, and you will be one. Nothing so indicates ill-breeding as a nervous, fidgetty, restless manner. The real lady or gentleman will be composed and undisturbed under every trying circumstance. They have taught themselves *self-control*, and this is readily learned by those with inclination and determination to learn.

2. *Go into Society.*—To learn to swim you must go into the water. To overcome the feeling of bashfulness, and to be at ease in company, you must go into company. On no account should you neglect this duty which you owe to yourself. Take every opportunity to attend balls, picnics, parties, sociables, etc., and always rank

yourself as one of the most desirable and popular young men of the occasion, and you will undoubtedly be so. Remember the fact that others will estimate you as you estimate yourself. And here we again repeat, *Do not be, or act, afraid of the girls.* They won't hurt you. Walk boldly up and make yourself agreeable. They will meet you half way. If at any time you feel a little fluttering of the heart, don't subside into a corner with the say-nothings and do-nothings, but "circulate around," and you will be surprised how easily you will find yourself at home and at ease, chatting with some nice people.

For removing Bashfulness, awkwardness, and all manner of similar disagreeable things, there could not possibly be a better place than the dancing-school. Young men who live away from villages, and who have but few, or no desirable associates outside the family circle, and who are distressingly awkward in speech and manner, if they can have a few terms at a dancing-school, will be so improved in address, manners, and general appearance as to surprise all who know them. We are acquainted with a person, now an old man, large, heavy, clumsy, who weighed one hundred and eighty pounds the day he was sixteen, and was six feet and an inch high. He was so awkward, to use his own statement, that he could hardly get into a room where there was company without hitting both sides of the door, and could scarcely sit down without knocking over his chair, knowing not what to do with his feet, his hands, nor himself. He chanced to have an opportunity to attend a dancing-school for three months—they were very uncommon in the locality where he resided—and he was there trained in the common civilities and courtesies of society; how to enter and leave a room, how to receive introductions, how to receive and dismiss company, etc. Though he is a farmer, not much used to society, there is to-day an easy, quiet grace, and a polish of manners that would pass anywhere acceptably; and he attributes it to the brief tuition in a dancing-school. While he may not remember much that he learned as a dancer, he remembers all that he learned that is necessary for performing the common courtesies of the parlor. So attend all the dances possible, and under all circumstances remember that you are a MAN and a GENTLEMAN.

Many often hesitate and become diffident from a lack of readiness in expressing their ideas, and from a fear that they do not speak correctly and elegantly. Now speaking grammatically is a mere matter of education. If lacking in this respect, the use of any good grammar, and particularly "COMPOSITION AND RHETORIC," already mentioned, with "LIVE AND LEARN;" or "1000 MISTAKES CORRECTED," will be all you require in this direction. "ONE THOUSAND MISTAKES CORRECTED," is better than half-a-dozen living teachers.

To express one's self with fluency in conversation is an art that can be acquired by a little practice, in adopting the method of the great orator Clay, in gaining quick readiness in speech. "I owe my success in life," said he, "chiefly to one circumstance—that at the age of twenty-seven I commenced, and continued for years the practice of daily reading and speaking upon the contents of some historical or scientific book. These off-hand efforts were made sometimes in a cornfield, at others in the forest, and not unfrequently in some distant barn, with the horse and the ox for my auditors. It is to this early practice of the art of all arts, that I am indebted for my subsequent destiny."

Reading aloud from some book, enunciating every word clearly and distinctly, with a dictionary at hand to settle instantly in your own mind any question as to the proper pronunciation of particular words, is a practice so abundantly fruitful of good results, that those who will practise it even for a short time, will scarcely be induced to relinquish it. In reading, cultivate the purely conversational tone. It is as easy to read as it is to talk, yet there are few good readers. The tone of voice, modulation, accent, etc., should be precisely as if you were in conversation, not as if you were preaching in a drawling, monotonous way. Read well and you will converse well, and both are superior accomplishments, acquired with facility; though the orator who pours forth his thoughts with such apparent ease, achieves his wonderful power only by means of patient labor, after much repetition, and, like Disraeli, often after bitter disappointments.

So take courage, young men, and if you have a difficulty to overcome, grapple with it at once; facility will come with practice, and strength and success with repeated effort. And always recollect, that the mind and character may be trained to almost perfect discipline, enabling it to move with a grace, spirit and freedom almost incomprehensible to those who have not subjected themselves to a similar training.

Take a raw recruit; he stoops, he walks in a shuffling, slouchy manner; he is painfully awkward. A few weeks under the Drill-Sergeant, and he walks forth erect, dignified, with the true soldierly bearing. Life seems but for the purpose of mere drilling. In one form or another we cannot escape it; neither should we desire to do so.

BASHFULNESS FROM IGNORANCE OF THE WAYS OF SOCIETY.

It is certainly very embarrassing and conducive of bashfulness to be thrust into a glittering room filled with people superior to one's self in position, and equally cultured in the knowledge of what is due to the place and occasion. A sensitive, uncultured man or maiden, with rustic garb and rustic speech, and little knowledge respecting correct manners, introduced at once to the presence of cultured ladies and gentlemen, does not know what to do with hands nor feet; whether to sit or to stand, or to hide. Is it to be wondered at that such a person acts and feels cheap and diminutive?

But, diffident reader, do not be discouraged, for general good breeding is very easy of attainment. You must possess simply *common sense, self-possession,* and a *habit of observation.*

The exercise of a good common sense will show you plainly enough what is right and wrong—what is proper and improper. Self-possession will prevent from doing awkward and bungling things; and by observation you will soon learn the manners of the well-bred.

"But I won't know how to act, mother," said a lad as he was about starting to his first party. "Keep your eyes open, and just do as the others do," was the answer, and better advice could not have been given.

Quiet self-possession will enable a person quite unacquainted with the usages of society to conduct himself very acceptably even in the most superior company. It is the foolish feeling of timidity that causes the trepidation and bashfulness, and consequent uneasy manners when in company, with the class of persons for whose benefit this book was written. *Why* should you be timid and backward, and show by your hesitating ways that you do not feel at ease? You surely can notice how those about you conduct themselves, and conduct yourself accordingly. Why should you not enter a room filled with company like any other well-bred person, in an easy, unconcerned manner, and addressing those about you, even those with whom you are not acquainted, without restraint, and without embarrassment? If you cannot muster sufficient spirit to do this, you had better turn travelling agent and call from house to house till you are not afraid of associating and conversing with strangers.

Yet to be well-bred without ceremony; easy without carelessness; self-possessed and dignified with modesty; polite without affectation; pleasing without servility; cheerful without being noisy; frank without indiscretion; and secret without mysteriousness; to know the proper time and place for whatever you say or do, and do it with the air of the well-bred—all this requires time and close observation. "MANNERS MAKE THE MAN." Old, but good. The power or influence of an easy, pleasing, deferential manner; of a polite, gracious and genteel address, is shown in a multitude of ways, and is acknowledged by high and low, and could not be better illustrated than by the success of great Counterfeiters, Forgers, and "Confidence men" generally. They are invariably men of the most polished and insinuating address. They listen to you with a consummate, well-bred air of interest and attention. They flatter you unconsciously, but none the less powerfully by the deep respect they apparently show to every word of your conversation; and when they address you it is as if to a person deserving of the highest consideration. And all this with such a combination of suavity, self-respect and dignity that it is most powerful to please. And these accomplished rascals have trained themselves to polished address and perfection of manners solely for the purpose of winning in their schemes with men.

Judicious flattery is incomparable as a means of pleasing. No person is proof against it, and one of its most delicate and effective forms is in showing a seeming deference to us—our conversation—opinions and advice. The ladies are particularly susceptible to polite and urbane manners. The act of a gentleman raising his hat and bowing gracefully to a lady, is really, or seemingly, a mark of esteem and respect, and the lady is pleased, as she should be. Little attentions thoughtfully shown are certain to please, and to secure that regard the person showing them is entitled to receive.

"He is a perfect gentleman," from a lady simply means that he has been generous in his gallant little attentions to her.

"A good listener,"—and how rare they are!—can not be otherwise than a thoughtful, sensible, and pleasing person. By his apparent deep interest in our conversation, he flatters our self-love; and whoever does that, without seeming intention, has advanced in our good opinion.

There is nothing so grossly rude, nor so little forgiven, as inattention from a person whom you are addressing. Many persons are so thoughtlessly or ignorantly rude, that while you are speaking to them, instead of looking at you with attention, they will look out of the window, into the fire, or up at the ceiling, and, it may be, speak to, or answer some other person, thus seeming to imply implicitly that the most trifling object deserves their attention more than anything you may be saying. The emphatic desire in every well-ordered mind to punish such an offensively ill-bred person we consider highly commendable.

In regard to the ways and usages of society we do not propose to say anything here, as they can be readily learned by observation, or from any of the several good books on the subject, mentioned in another place.

BASHFULNESS FROM ILL-DRESS.

A person may have the education of a College President, and possess the wealth of an Astor, yet let him with soiled or slouchy clothes be suddenly brought into the society of ladies and gentlemen, and he will feel and act constrained and bashful in spite of his best endeavors.

Let a well-bred, well-dressed person make a call and discover, when it is too late, that his boots are muddy, or his finger-nails not cleaned, and he will inevitably act ill at ease, and be glad when he is safe in the street again.

A mechanic going home at night in his work-day clothes, with traces of toil on hands and face, walks along with the well-dressed crowd in a subdued and humble manner. The same mechanic, two hours later, thoroughly washed and shaved, and arrayed in his best holiday clothes, taking his wife to a place of amusement, perhaps, has the appearance of another man. He walks with an erect and manly air, and feels that he is a man among men.

The question of dress is one of the utmost importance. It often determines our characters and our success in life. A person meanly dressed will feel meanly and act meanly. Everybody has experienced the sudden and agreeable change in one's feelings from merely changing from an old, poor suit of clothes to a new one. The dogs, with amazing instinct, look upon the ragged beggar with suspicion, and meet him with growls and snaps, while the well-dressed gentleman coming up the walk, is welcomed with friendly wags of the tail.

> "Costly thy habit, as thy purse can buy,
> But not expressed in fancy; rich, not gaudy,
> For the apparel oft proclaims the man."

This, from Shakespeare, is sound advice. City people, including those who are in far more moderate circumstances than even the small farmers, are far better dressed than the average of country people. The farmer's wife going out for an evening's visit, or to church, "fixes up," and makes a presentable appearance. The farmer going to town, ten miles away, shaves, puts on his best suit, and feels respectable. They are going into company—going to meet with people. On other days there seems to be little regard for personal appearance as far as dress is concerned. Now a resident of a city is always in company. He is on perpetual exhibition. He is classed as he is dressed; if like a beggar, then a beggar; if like a gentleman—a gentleman.

Now, young and diffident reader, we insist that you can never rid yourself of the bashful feeling while in company so long as you are poorly dressed. By "poorly" we do not refer to the material, only to the style and shape. A person may wear pantaloons and coat of the finest broadcloth, but if they are baggy and slouchy, will he be considered well dressed? Coarse material for coat and trousers have been popular for several years past, and a good suit of clothes can be bought at moderate cost. If you live within a reasonable distance of a city, always buy your clothes there, as you will be sure to have them in the latest style—that is, if you notice what the style is. Never select pantaloons with large checks or stripes. Light brown, or dark material is the most becoming. If you are obliged to have your clothes made in the country, have them cut, if possible, by a tailor. It don't so much matter who makes them up.

The fit of a collar adds to or mars a person's appearance greatly. It should turn down and both ends nearly meet at the buttonhole. A small brown or black tie, with the ends tucked under the collar, or a plain, narrow silk tie, or one of small white and black checks, will be neat and becoming. A large neck-tie of a flaming color, so often worn by country youths, is a prominent sign of an uncultivated taste.

THE HAIR, ETC.—City men, young and old, are very particular about having their hair kept neatly and closely cut. Why those in the country seem to delight in shocks of long hair we never could see; and we lived in the country twenty years. Don't do it. Cultivate personal neatness insiduously, and give an indication of it by keeping your hair neatly trimmed. Don't let neighbor Smith do it with his sheep shears, thereby saving a shilling or two; but go to a professional barber, even if he is in the next town.

THE TEETH require particular attention. Use a tooth-pick always after eating, rinsing the mouth at the same time. Scrub the teeth thoroughly morning and night with a tooth-brush rubbed on a bit of soap. There is no excuse for not doing this; a good brush will cost twenty cents, and the time occupied about six minutes a day! The feeling of purity and comfort experienced will amply recompense you for the trifling trouble. Take a hot bath as often as you can, using soap and brush freely; and be certain that no disagreeable fœtid odor comes from your feet from want of cleanliness.

That you would go into the presence of ladies with soiled hands is not probable, but be careful to notice that the nails are scrupulously clean.

These various little attentions towards personal neatness and comeliness will soon become a second nature. And after you have instituted these reforms in regard to your toilet, etc., you will not fail to observe that you are treated with a much greater respect and consideration, especially by the ladies, than before. Your own estimation of yourself has greatly increased, and you find that the miserable bashful feeling formerly experienced when in the society of those you considered your superiors, no longer troubles you.

It is important for those young men who are apt to disparage themselves in comparison with their wealthy acquaintances, to bear in mind that riches and rank have no necessary connection with genuine gentlemanly qualities. The poor man may be a true gentleman in spirit and in daily life. He may be honest, truthful, polite, temperate, courageous, self-respecting, and self-helping—that is, *a true gentleman*. The poor man with a rich spirit, is always superior to the rich man with a mean spirit.

BASHFULNESS CAUSED BY ILL HEALTH.

A person who has any noticeable physical deformity, or who has been reduced by certain nervous diseases, cannot be expected to possess that buoyancy and manliness of spirit that he would were circumstances different. Persons with nerves that are naturally excitable, will greatly increase their excitability by the habitual use of strong tea, etc. As a result, they are nervous, fidgetty, and never quite at ease. When in company they easily lose their self-possession and do blundering things generally. There are certain habits known to young men that cause a person to become bashful and sheep-faced to a surprising degree.

We have no particular suggestions to offer where diffidence and bashfulness are the result of prolonged illness or disease. Every means should be taken to restore the health; and with the restoration will come the old manly and courageous spirit.

When the nerves are weak and unsteady from physical debility, great benefit will be immediately derived, in the majority of cases, from the use, for two or three weeks at a time, of *Iodoform*, two or three grains a day—taken at meal time on a bit of moist bread.

In case the voice and lungs are weak, read aloud daily, enunciating every word clearly and distinctly. Commence by reading ten minutes at a time, and finally half an hour. You will soon acquire a richness and depth of tone to be proud of, besides greatly improving your health by increasing the capacity of the lungs.

TO PASTE INSIDE YOUR HAT.

—And these few precepts in thy memory
Hold fast: "Give thy thoughts no tongue,
Nor any unproportion'd thought his act.

Be thou familiar, but by no means vulgar
To the friends thou hast, and their adoption tried,
Grapple them to thy soul with hooks of steel:
Beware of entrance to a quarrel; but, being in, bear
It, that the opposer may beware of thee.

Give every man thine ear, but few thy voice;
Neither a borrower, nor a lender be,
For loan oft loses both itself and friend.

This above all:—To thine own self be true;
And it must follow, as the night the day,
Thou can'st not be false to any man."

TRUTHS REPEATED.

Secrecy is a characteristic of good breeding. A gentleman or lady will never tell in one company what they see or hear in another; much less divert the present company at the expense of the last. In conversation there is generally a tacit reliance that what is said will not be repeated. Tattlers are contemptable.

Whispering in company is an act of unmistakable ill-breeding. It seems to imply that neither the persons whom we do not wish should hear are unworthy our confidence, or that we are speaking improperly of them.

Incessant talkers are very disagreeable companions. Nothing can be more rude than to engross the conversation to yourself, or to take the words, as it were, out of another person's mouth. All generally like to bear their part in a conversation, and for one to monopolize it, is a tacit acknowledgment that he considers his conversation of more importance, or more interesting than that of others. Long talkers are unmitigated bores.

Giving advice unasked is an impertinence. It is, in effect, declaring ourselves wiser than those to whom we give it; reproaching them with ignorance and inexperience. It is a freedom that ought not to be taken with any common acquaintance.

It is true politeness not to interrupt a person in a story, whether you have heard it before or not.

Men repent speaking ten times, for once they repent keeping silence.

You will be reckoned by the world nearly of the same character with those whose company you keep.

If you give yourself a loose tongue in company, you may almost depend on being pulled to pieces as soon as your back is turned, however they may seem entertained with your conversation.

It is ill manners to trouble people with talking too much either of yourself or your affairs. If you are full of yourself, consider that you, and your affairs, are not so interesting to other people as to you.

Lector House believes that a society develops through a two-fold approach of continuous learning and adaptation, which is derived from the study of classic literary works spread across the historic timeline of literature records. Therefore, we aim at reviving, repairing and redeveloping all those inaccessible or damaged but historically as well as culturally important literature across subjects so that the future generations may have an opportunity to study and learn from past works to embark upon a journey of creating a better future.

This book is a result of an effort made by Lector House towards making a contribution to the preservation and repair of original ancient works which might hold historical significance to the approach of continuous learning across subjects.

HAPPY READING & LEARNING!

LECTOR HOUSE LLP
E-MAIL: lectorpublishing@gmail.com